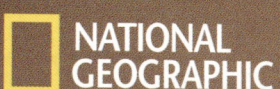

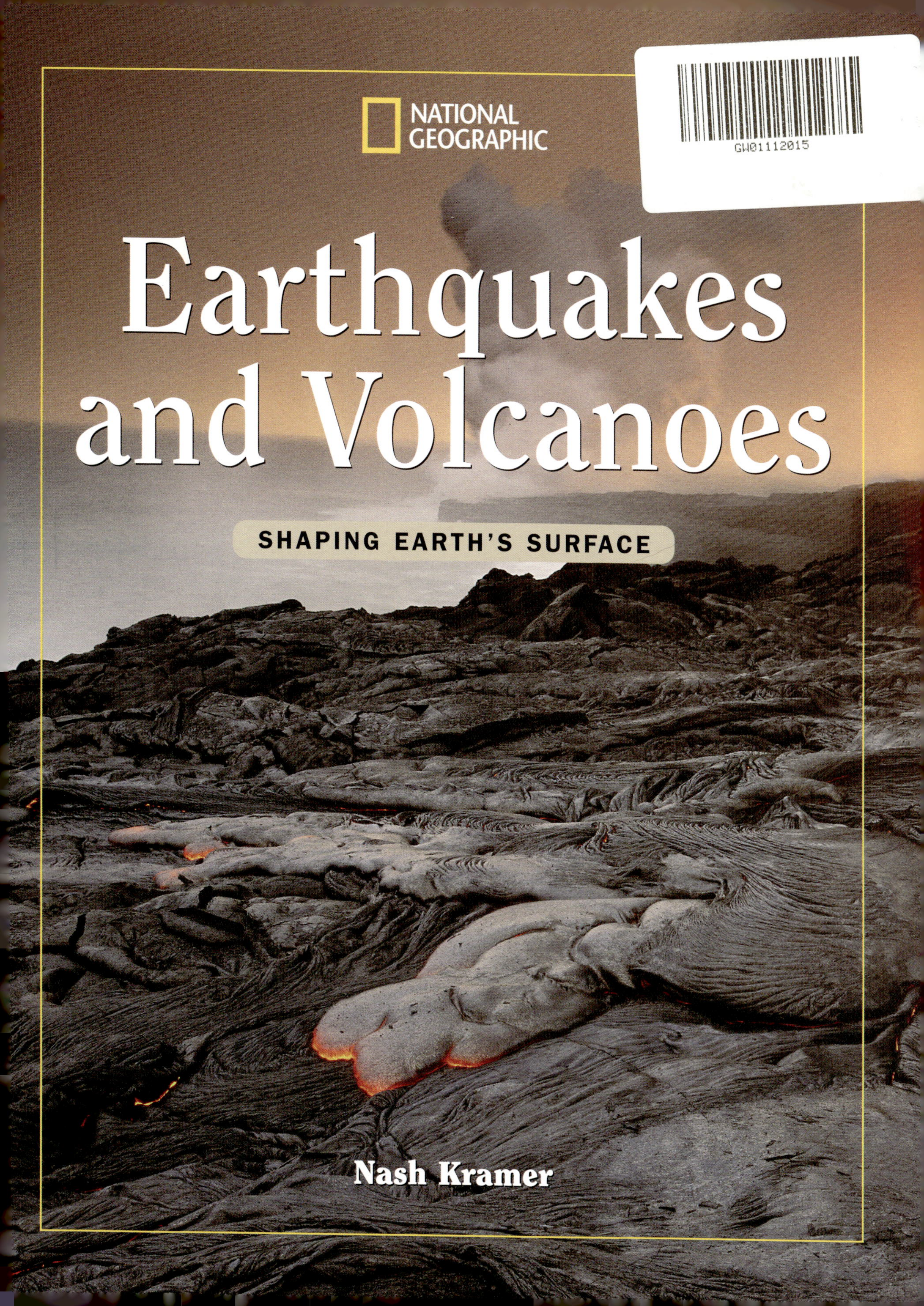

NATIONAL GEOGRAPHIC

Earthquakes and Volcanoes

SHAPING EARTH'S SURFACE

Nash Kramer

PICTURE CREDITS

Cover: photograph of Puu Oo Crater erupting © Jim Sugar/Corbis/Tranz.

Photographs: page 1 © Gavriel Jecan/Corbis/Tranz; page 4 (bottom left), Corbis; page 4 (bottom right), Photodisc; page 5 (top) © Roger Ressmeyer/Corbis/Tranz; page 5 (bottom left), Photodisc; page 5 (bottom right), Corbis; page 6 © Gary Braasch/Corbis/Tranz; page 7 © Wolfgang Kaehler/Corbis/Tranz; page 9 © Lloyd Cluff/Corbis/Tranz; page 10, Corbis; page 11 © Reuters; page 12 © Roger Ressmeyer/Corbis/Tranz; page 14 © Reuters; pages 15–16 © Roger Ressmeyer/Corbis/Tranz; page 21 © photograph of the Hawaiian Islands seen from space, courtesy NASA; page 24 © Roger Ressmeyer/Corbis/Tranz; page 25 © Neil Rabinowitz/Corbis/Tranz; page 26 © David Muench/Corbis/Tranz; page 29 © Seth Joel/Taxi/Getty Images.

Illustration on page 13 by Elena Petrov.

Produced through the worldwide resources of the National Geographic Society, John M. Fahey, Jr., President and Chief Executive Officer; Gilbert M. Grosvenor, Chairman of the Board.

PREPARED BY NATIONAL GEOGRAPHIC SCHOOL PUBLISHING
Sheron Long, Chief Executive Officer; Samuel Gesumaria, President; Steve Mico, Executive Vice President and Publisher; Francis Downey, Editor in Chief; Richard Easby, Editorial Manager; Margaret Sidlosky, Director of Design and Illustrations; Jim Hiscott, Design Manager; Cynthia Olson and Ruth Ann Thompson, Art Directors; Matt Wascavage, Director of Publishing Services; Lisa Pergolizzi, Production Manager.

MANUFACTURING AND QUALITY CONTROL
Christopher A. Liedel, Chief Financial Officer; Phillip L. Schlosser, Vice President; Clifton M. Brown III, Director.

EDITOR
Mary Anne Wengel

PROGRAMME CONSULTANTS
Dr. Shirley V. Dickson, National Literacy Consultant; James A. Shymansky, E. Desmond Lee Professor of Science Education, University of Missouri-St Louis.

Copyright © 2007 Macmillan Education Australia.

First published in 2007 in Great Britain by Kingscourt/McGraw-Hill publishers.

McGraw-Hill International (UK) Limited
McGraw-Hill House
Shoppenhangers Road, Maidenhead
Berkshire, SL6 2QL

www.kingscourt.co.uk

The materials in this publication may be photocopied for use only within the purchasing organisation. Otherwise, all rights reserved and no part of the publication may be reproduced, stored in a retrieval system or transmitted, in any form, or by any means, electronic, mechanical, photocopying, recording or otherwise, without prior permission of the publishers. National Geographic, National Geographic Explorer, and the Yellow Border are trademarks of the National Geographic Society.

ISBN–13: 978-1-4202-1786-5

Printed in Hong Kong.

2011 2010 2009 2008 2007
1 2 3 4 5 6 7 8 9 10 11 12 13 14 15

Contents

- Shaping Earth's Surface....................4
- The Effects of Earthquakes and Volcanoes.......6
- Think About the Key Concepts..............17

Visual Literacy
Cutaway Diagram........................18

Genre Study
Cause and Effect Article....................20

The Creation of Hawaii....................21

- Apply the Key Concepts....................27

Research and Write
Write Your Own Cause and Effect Article......28

Glossary................................31

Index..................................32

Shaping Earth's Surface

Think of all the shapes and forms you can see on Earth's surface. These shapes and forms change all the time. Some changes happen quickly, as when an earthquake or volcano jolts the land. Other changes are slow, as when wind, water, or ice wears away rock. Wind, water, ice, earthquakes, and volcanoes are all forces that shape Earth's surface.

Key Concepts

1. Different forces shape the landforms that make up Earth's surface.
2. Earth's surface changes in different ways.
3. People try to control, or at least understand, the effect of forces that shape Earth's surface.

Forces Shaping Earth's Surface

Wind

Wind can change the surface of rock, deserts, plains, and coastlines.

Water

Water can change the landscape by carving out canyons and valleys.

In this book you will learn how earthquakes and volcanoes like this one shape Earth's surface.

Ice

Ice can slowly change the shape of rock and create new landforms.

Earthquakes and Volcanoes

Earthquakes and volcanoes can build landforms and destroy them.

The Effects of Earthquakes and Volcanoes

Earthquakes and **volcanoes** cause sudden dramatic changes to Earth's surface. Powerful earthquakes shake the ground violently. They can make enormous cracks in Earth's surface. They can even change the course of rivers. Volcanoes bring rivers of red-hot melted rock to Earth's surface. They can cause mountains to form or to crumble.

Earthquakes and volcanoes are among the most destructive natural events on Earth. They are both activated by strong movement within Earth's crust. The effects of earthquakes and volcanoes are visible immediately after they happen. They can cause huge damage to lives and property. They can also permanently alter the shape of the land.

The volcano of Mount St. Helens erupting in 1980

Key Concept 1 Different forces shape the landforms that make up Earth's surface.

Earth's Surface

Earth's surface is made up of rocks and soils that form its outer layer. These rocks and soils make up **landforms**. These landforms include mountains, valleys, deserts, and plains. They give Earth's surface its shape.

landforms
natural shapes on Earth's surface

Different **forces** change the shape of Earth's surface. Some forces, such as **weathering** and **erosion**, change Earth's surface slowly, over a long period of time. Weathering is the wearing away of rock. Erosion is the moving of rock and soil from one place to another.

forces
causes of movement and change

By comparison, volcanoes and earthquakes are forces that can change Earth's surface very quickly. In a matter of minutes or hours, earthquakes and volcanoes can dramatically alter landforms.

Koryak Volcano in Russia

Key Concept 2 Earth's surface changes in different ways.

Origins of Earthquakes and Volcanoes

Both earthquakes and volcanoes originate from natural forces within Earth's interior. They are both related to the movement of giant plates that make up Earth's surface.

Earth's surface is not a single piece of rock. It is broken into many pieces called **tectonic plates**. There are eight major tectonic plates and several small ones. These plates fit together like jigsaw pieces. The map below shows the boundaries of the major tectonic plates.

Tectonic plates usually move very slowly—only a few centimeters a year. They move in different directions so the movement of one tectonic plate affects those next to it. Some tectonic plates push toward each other, some pull apart from each other, and others slide past each other.

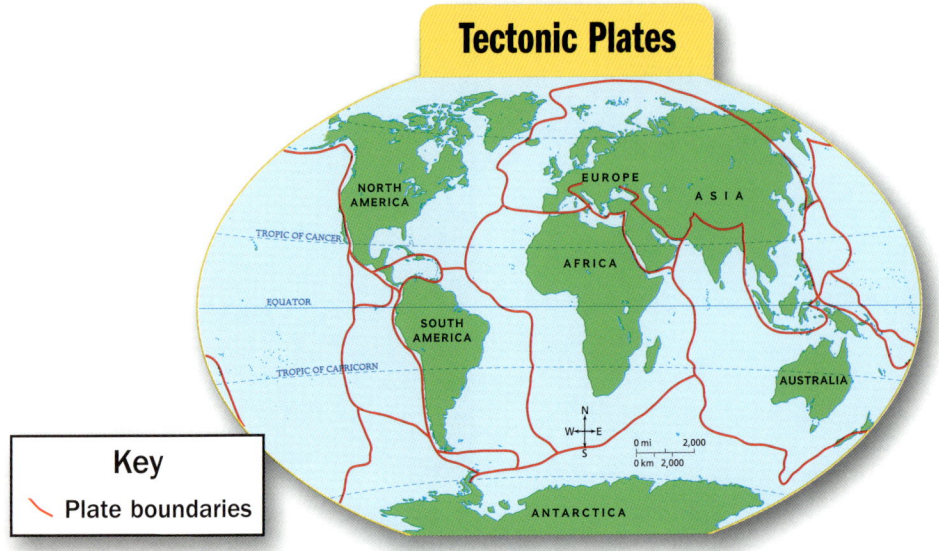

Tectonic Plates

Key
— Plate boundaries

What Causes an Earthquake? Earthquakes happen when the tectonic plates move suddenly and quickly. This sudden shift in the rock shakes all of the ground around it. Earthquakes can often be felt over large areas. They usually last less than a minute. The force of an earthquake can be so strong that it can cause huge landslides and the surface of Earth to crack.

As the tectonic plates scrape past each other, the pushing causes breaks, or **faults**, in Earth's surface. Faults may range in length from a few millimeters to thousands of kilometers. Many earthquakes occur along the tectonic plate boundaries. They can also occur in the middle of a tectonic plate, where faults also form. Earthquakes along this type of fault are much less frequent and much weaker than those along tectonic plate boundaries.

People inspecting earthquake damage in California

What Causes a Volcano? Powerful forces beneath Earth's surface also cause volcanoes. Volcanoes are openings through which red-hot materials from beneath Earth's surface erupt onto land. Volcanoes occur in an area of extreme volcanic activity in or between tectonic plates, called a **hotspot**.

Magma is the red-hot melted rock under Earth's surface. Volcanoes form and erupt when pressure inside Earth forces the magma toward the surface. The pressure and the heat cause the magma to blast through a **vent**, or opening, in the surface. A weakness in a tectonic plate can also become a vent if the weak part is over a hotspot.

When magma erupts through a vent in the surface, it becomes **lava**. Besides lava, gases, ash, and rock fragments may also be expelled from the volcano. Lava cools as it builds up around the opening and becomes hard rock. Over time, this cooled and hardened lava forms a cone-shaped mound or mountain.

Mount Fuji in Japan is a cone-shaped volcano formed from lava.

How Earthquakes and Volcanoes Change Earth's Surface

Earthquakes and volcanoes both dramatically change Earth's surface, though they do so in very different ways.

Changes Caused by Earthquakes Earthquakes are very common. Most cannot be felt. However, some earthquakes are so strong that they make great changes to the shape of Earth's surface. For example, when two plates push against each other the ground shakes. The land where the plates meet may crumple and buckle.

The shaking ground during an earthquake can also trigger landslides. The shaking loosens the soil on a slope and causes it to slide. As the ground shifts during an earthquake, rock movement can open up huge cracks in the ground and make rivers change their course. In 2001, there was a massive earthquake in the state of Gujarat in India. It caused cracks and forced underground water to the surface.

Huge cracks in the ground caused by the earthquake in Gujarat, India

Changes Caused by Volcanoes Volcanoes can change Earth's surface very quickly. They can both destroy landforms and create new ones. Some volcanic eruptions are so violent that they can blow a mountain apart. In 1980, when Mount St. Helens erupted, the north face of the mountain collapsed in a massive landslide. The top 305 meters (1,000 feet) of the mountain were blown away.

Volcano eruptions can also create new land. For example, the Hawaiian Islands are volcanoes that formed in the middle of the Pacific Plate, the tectonic plate that is covered by the Pacific Ocean. The volcanoes begin on the ocean floor. Over time, they build up and eventually emerge above sea level and form an island.

Eruptions change Earth's surface by covering the surrounding land with lava, ash, or mud that can be many meters deep. Lava from eruptions can also extend the coastline of a volcanic island.

Lava from Kilauea, a volcano in Hawaii

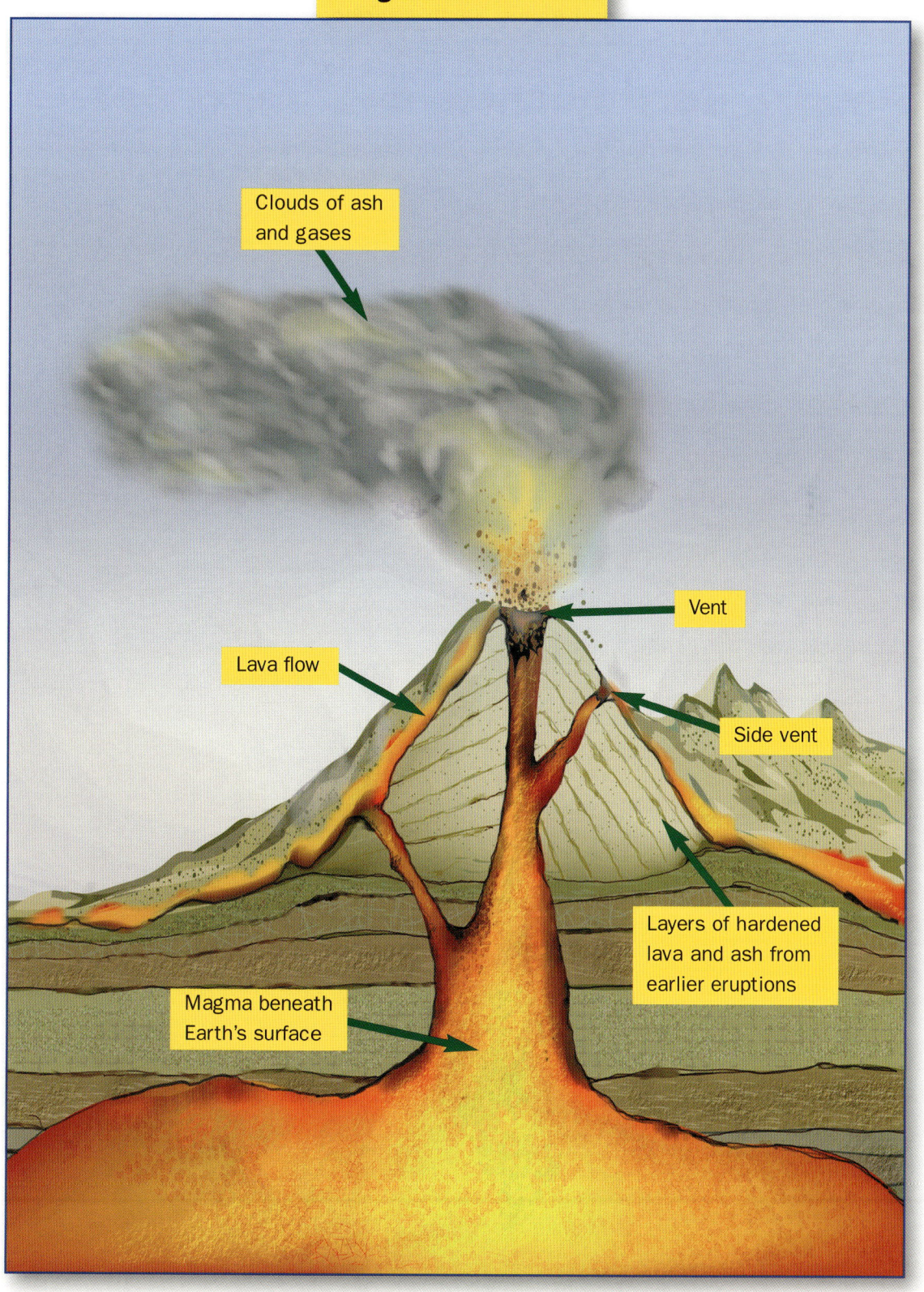

Key Concept 3 People try to control, or at least understand, the effect of forces that shape Earth's surface.

People, Earthquakes, and Volcanoes

Earthquakes and volcanoes can affect people's lives by causing widespread damage to buildings, crops, and water systems. People can also lose their lives because of earthquakes and volcanoes. People cannot control earthquakes and volcanoes. But, by studying their **effects**, they can learn ways to limit loss of life and damage to property.

effects
changes caused by the action of forces

Studying Earthquakes A **seismologist** is a person who studies earthquakes and how they affect Earth. Seismologists examine what happens to Earth during earthquakes. Seismologists use a tool called a seismograph to measure and record **seismic waves**. These are shock waves that come from the center of an earthquake. Seismic waves move through Earth like ripples over a pond.

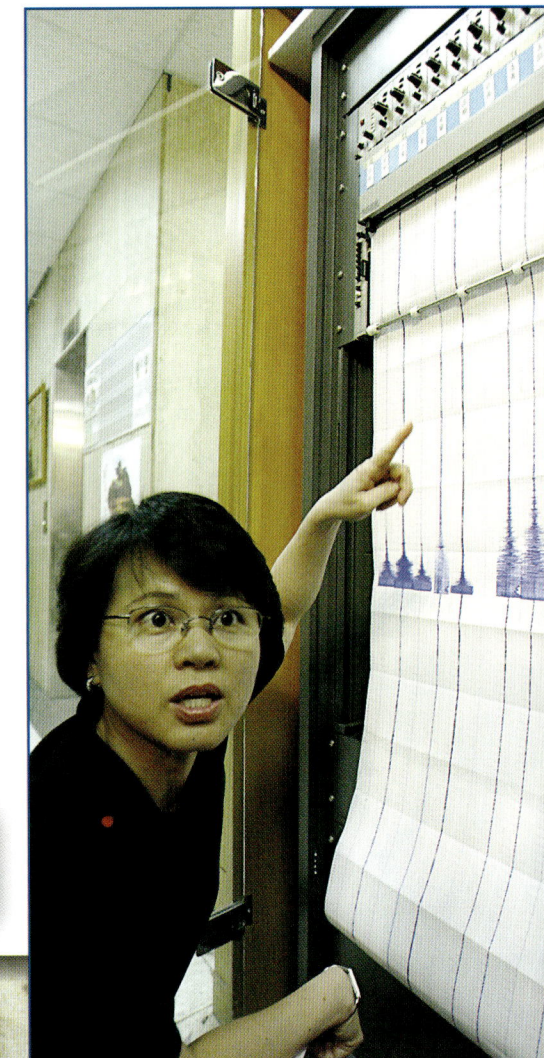

A seismologist points to an earthquake recorded on a seismograph.

Earthquake detection can alert seismologists to new faults in Earth. This way they will know where earthquakes may happen in the future. Although they can detect when earthquakes are happening, seismologists cannot yet predict when an earthquake will occur.

Small tremors occur all the time, but every few months a major earthquake occurs somewhere in the world. In areas where earthquakes are likely, knowing where to build and how to build can help minimize damage. Rubber pads beneath the foundations of buildings can absorb some of the shocks coming from the ground. Water and gas lines can have strong joints that bend but do not break. People can build houses and bridges with extra bracing so they are stronger and do not collapse during an earthquake.

People test a system for strengthening buildings on a model of a house.

Studying Volcanoes Scientists called **volcanologists** study volcanoes to try to find out why and when they will erupt. Volcanologists hope to learn how to predict volcanic eruptions. If they can do this, they can warn people and limit the damage and loss of life that volcanoes can cause.

Volcanologists know that certain signs may indicate that an eruption is likely. Gases escape from volcano craters, and earthquakes occur before most eruptions. However, volcanologists still cannot be certain if, or when, an eruption will happen. They can estimate that it may happen within hours or days, but an accurate prediction is still not possible.

Learning about volcanoes is important. People who live near volcanoes need to know what to do if there is an eruption. Accurate prediction of eruptions would mean people could be evacuated from an area in time. Volcanologists continue to study volcanoes, hoping to learn more about them.

A volcanologist taking a sample of hot lava from a lava flow

Think About the Key Concepts

Think about what you read. Think about the pictures and the diagram. Use these to answer the questions. Share what you think with others.

1. Explain two ways that forces change Earth's surface.

2. Explain the difference between weathering and erosion.

3. In what ways can people be affected by the forces that shape Earth's surface?

4. In what ways can people control the effects of forces that shape Earth's surface?

Cutaway Diagram

Diagrams are pictures that show information.
You can learn new ideas without having to read many words. Diagrams use pictures and words to explain ideas.

There are different kinds of diagrams.
This diagram of how an island forms over a hotspot is a **cutaway diagram**. A cutaway diagram is a three-dimensional picture that shows a "slice" of something, such as a slice of Earth. Look back at the diagram on page 13. It is a cutaway diagram of a volcano.

How to Read a Diagram

1. **Read the title.**
   The title tells you what the diagram is about.
2. **Read the labels.**
   Labels point out the important parts of the diagram.
3. **Study the diagram.**
   Which parts of the diagram are on the surface, and which parts are beneath the surface?
4. **Think about what you learned.**
   What did the cutaway diagram show you?

How an Island Forms over a Hotspot

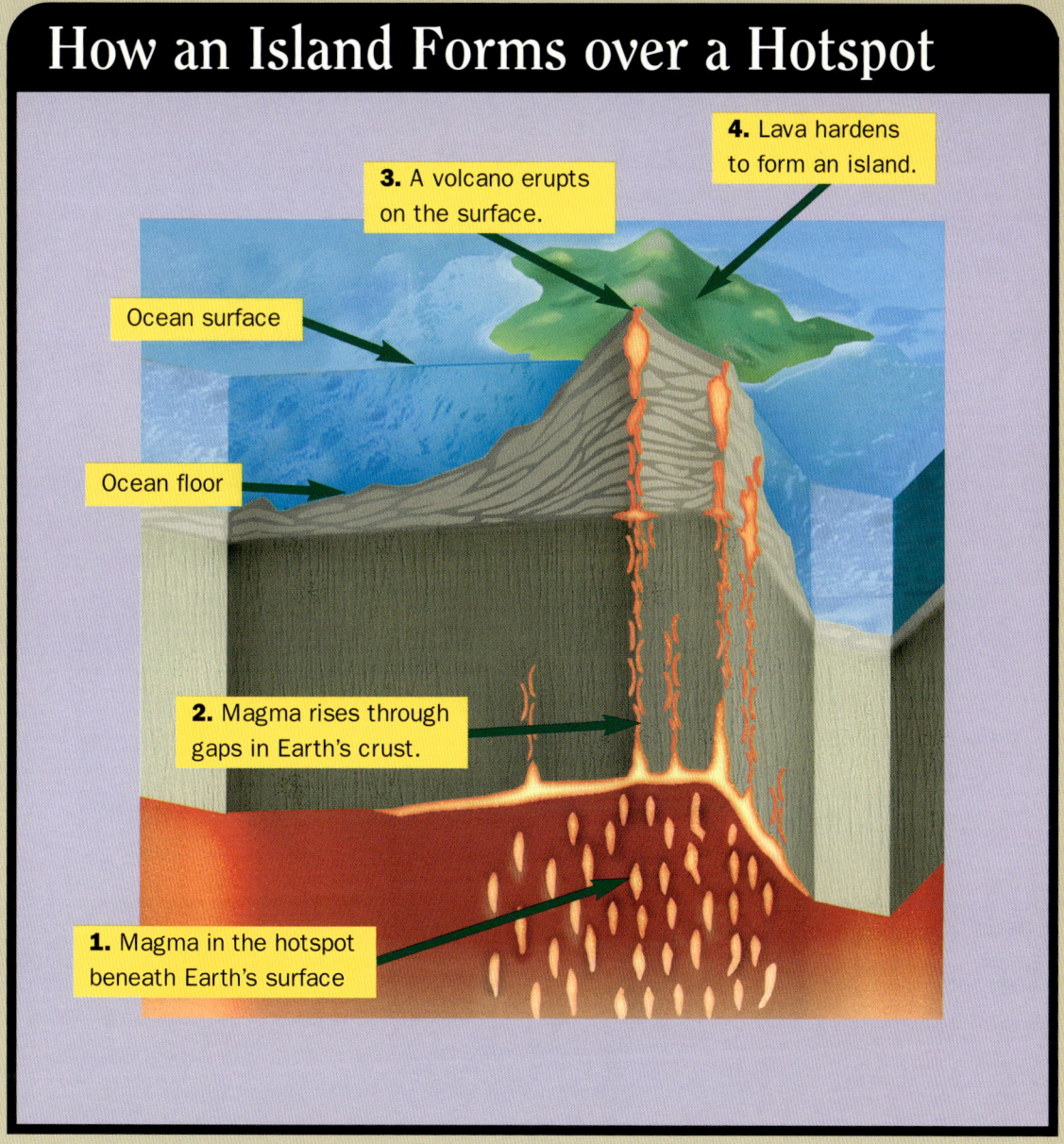

What Did You Learn?

Read the diagram by following the steps on page 18. Write a short paragraph explaining what you learned. Then exchange paragraphs with a classmate. See if your paragraphs are clear to each other.

GENRE STUDY

Cause and Effect Article

Cause and effect articles may describe an event. They tell why the event happened (the causes) and the results of the event (the effects). The article starting on page 21 describes the volcanoes of Hawaii.

Cause and effect articles generally include the following:

The Creation of Hawaii

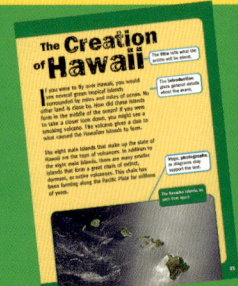

The Introduction

The introduction gives general details about the event that will be described in the article.

The Volcanoes That Caused Hawaii to Form

Effects of the Volcanoes

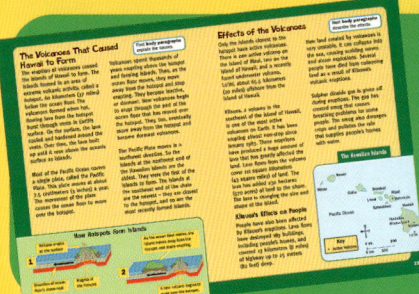

The Body Paragraphs

The first few body paragraphs explain the causes and the next paragraphs describe the effects.

The Future of the Hawaiian Islands

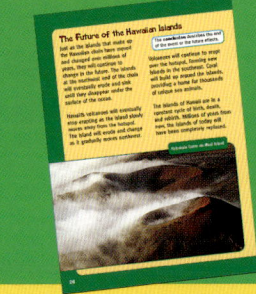

The Conclusion

The conclusion explains how the event ended or describes possible future effects.

The Creation of Hawaii

The **title** tells what the article will be about.

If you were to fly over Hawaii, you would see several green tropical islands surrounded by miles and miles of ocean. No other land is close by. How did these islands form in the middle of the ocean? If you were to take a closer look down, you might see a smoking volcano. The volcano gives a clue to what caused the Hawaiian Islands to form.

The **introduction** gives general details about the event.

The eight main islands that make up the state of Hawaii are the tops of volcanoes. In addition to the eight main islands, there are many smaller islands that form a great chain of extinct, dormant, or active volcanoes. This chain has been forming along the Pacific Plate for millions of years.

Maps, **photographs**, or diagrams may support the text.

The Hawaiian Islands, as seen from space

The Volcanoes That Caused Hawaii to Form

> First **body paragraphs** explain the causes.

The eruption of volcanoes caused the islands of Hawaii to form. The islands formed over an area of extreme volcanic activity, called a hotspot, 60 kilometers (37 miles) below the ocean floor. The volcanoes formed when hot, flowing lava from the hotspot burst through vents in Earth's surface. On the surface, the lava cooled and hardened around the vents. Over time, the lava built up until it rose above the ocean's surface as islands.

Most of the Pacific Ocean covers a single plate, called the Pacific Plate. This plate moves at about 7.5 centimeters (3 inches) a year. The movement of the plate causes the ocean floor to move over the hotspot.

Volcanoes spend thousands of years erupting above the hotspot and forming islands. Then, as the ocean floor moves, they move away from the hotspot and stop erupting. They become inactive, or dormant. New volcanoes begin to erupt through the part of the ocean floor that has moved over the hotspot. They, too, eventually move away from the hotspot and become dormant volcanoes.

The Pacific Plate moves in a northwest direction. So the islands at the northwest end of the Hawaiian Islands are the oldest. They were the first of the islands to form. The islands at the southeast end of the chain are the newest—they are closest to the hotspot, and so are the most recently formed islands.

How Hotspots Form Islands

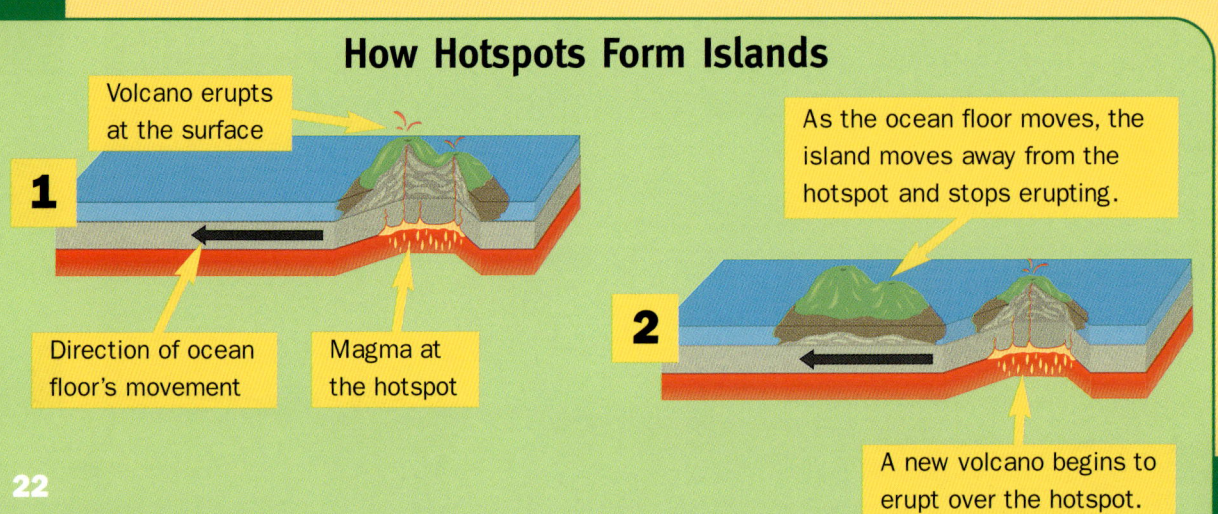

1. Volcano erupts at the surface. Direction of ocean floor's movement. Magma at the hotspot.
2. As the ocean floor moves, the island moves away from the hotspot and stops erupting. A new volcano begins to erupt over the hotspot.

Effects of the Volcanoes

> Next **body paragraphs** describe the effects.

Only the islands closest to the hotspot have active volcanoes. There is one active volcano on the island of Maui, two on the island of Hawaii, and a recently found underwater volcano, Lo'ihi, about 65.5 kilometers (20 miles) offshore from the island of Hawaii.

Kilauea, a volcano in the southeast of the island of Hawaii, is one of the most active volcanoes on Earth. It has been erupting almost nonstop since January 1983. These eruptions have produced a huge amount of lava that has greatly affected the land. Lava flows from the volcano cover 111 square kilometers (43 square miles) of land. The lava has added 230 hectares (570 acres) of land to the shore. The lava is changing the size and shape of the island.

Kilauea's Effects on People

People have also been affected by Kilauea's eruptions. Lava flows have destroyed 189 buildings, including people's homes, and covered 13 kilometers (8 miles) of highway up to 25 meters (82 feet) deep.

New land created by volcanoes is very unstable. It can collapse into the sea, causing scalding waves and steam explosions. Several people have died from collapsing land as a result of Kilauea's volcanic eruptions.

Sulphur dioxide gas is given off during eruptions. The gas has created smog that causes breathing problems for some people. The smog also damages crops and pollutes the rain that supplies people's homes with water.

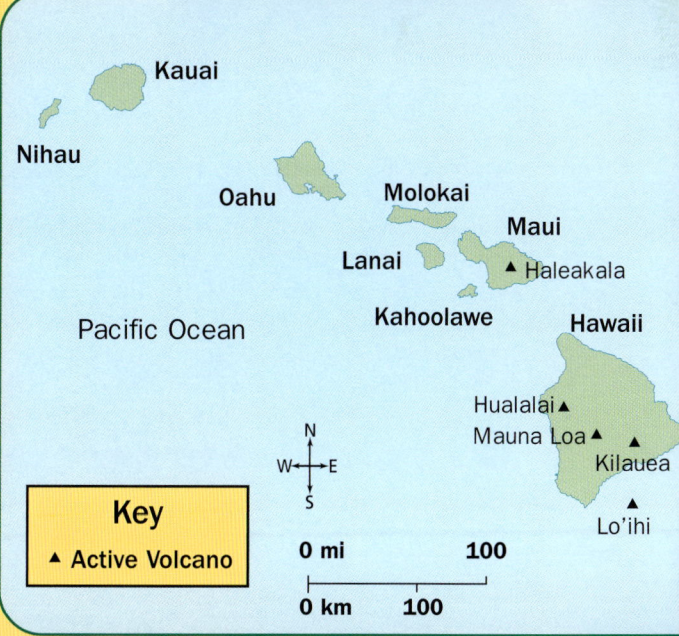

The Hawaiian Islands

A Changing Appearance

The Hawaiian Islands are formed from volcanic lava and ash. When an island is still over the hotspot, erupting volcanoes will add new lava and ash to the island. The island of Hawaii is over the hotspot right now. Its volcanoes are still erupting and adding new lava to the land. Hawaii is also the youngest island. It is less than a million years old.

When an island moves away from the hotspot, its volcanoes no longer erupt. No more lava and ash are added to the land. The forces of weathering and erosion now dramatically change the landscape.

Rock made from lava and ash is soft and easily weathered by rain, wind, and the ocean. Over time, these forces wear down the islands.

The oldest Hawaiian Islands are also the smallest islands. For instance, the island of Kure would have been as big as the island of Hawaii 25 million years ago. But the forces of weathering and erosion have ground it down so much that it has now disappeared. All that is left is a ring of coral and sand that is just a few meters above sea level.

A volcanologist watching lava flow from Kilauea

Coral Reefs

Many of the Hawaiian Islands are surrounded by coral reefs. Coral reefs form over thousands of years from the skeletons of sea creatures, such as algae, coral, snails, and urchins. These sea creatures make their homes on the volcanoes when they are still deep below the surface of the ocean.

Over time, the skeletons of the sea creatures compact together to form a large, hard mass of coral. Large areas of coral are called coral reefs. The reefs around the northwestern Hawaiian Islands are made up of some kinds of coral that are found nowhere else in the world. The reefs are home to many kinds of fish and seabirds that are unique to Hawaii.

From Islands to Atolls

The volcanic islands are very heavy, so they are slowly sinking. This sinking, along with erosion, means that the islands will eventually disappear under the ocean. Over millions of years, the erosion of volcanic islands combined with slow sinking causes the islands to disappear under the ocean. When an island erodes away and sinks beneath the ocean, often an atoll is left behind. An atoll is a ring-shaped coral reef that once formed around a volcanic island. An atoll rises above the ocean's surface as a kind of island. Many islands found in the northwestern end of the Hawaiian Islands are now atolls.

The coral reefs in Hawaii attract many tourists.

The Future of the Hawaiian Islands

Just as the islands that make up the Hawaiian chain have moved and changed over millions of years, they will continue to change in the future. The islands at the northwest end of the chain will eventually erode and sink until they disappear under the surface of the ocean.

Hawaii's volcanoes will eventually stop erupting as the island slowly moves away from the hotspot. The island will erode and change as it gradually moves northwest.

> The **conclusion** describes the end of the event or the future effects.

Volcanoes will continue to erupt over the hotspot, forming new islands in the southeast. Coral will build up around the islands, providing a home for thousands of unique sea animals.

The islands of Hawaii are in a constant cycle of birth, death, and rebirth. Millions of years from now, the islands of today will have been completely replaced.

Haleakala Crater on Maui Island

Apply the Key Concepts

Key Concept 1 Different forces shape the landforms that make up Earth's surface.

Activity Draw a landscape with different landforms that are found on Earth's surface. Label the different landforms in your drawing.

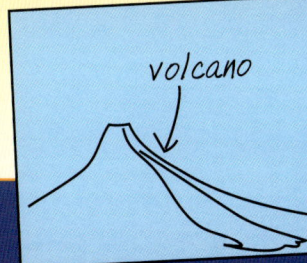

volcano

Key Concept 2 Earth's surface changes in different ways.

Activity Choose an example of changes brought about by an earthquake or a volcano. Then draw a simple diagram to show the steps in the process.

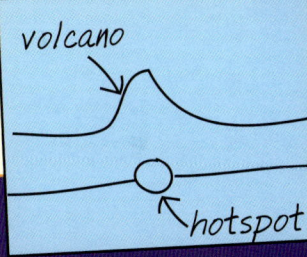

volcano

hotspot

Key Concept 3 People try to control, or at least understand, the effect of forces that change Earth's surface.

Activity Imagine you are a person affected by an earthquake or a volcano. Write a letter to a friend describing the changes brought about by the earthquake or volcano and how it has affected you.

Dear Mary,

RESEARCH AND WRITE

Write Your Own Cause and Effect Article

You have read the cause and effect article about an event in nature. Now you will write your own cause and effect article about an event you find interesting.

1. Study the Model

Look back at the description of cause and effect articles on page 20. Then read the introduction. What does it tell you about the topic? Read the body text. Think about how the information under the heading *The Volcanoes That Caused Hawaii to Form* is different from the information under the heading *Effects of the Volcanoes*. Now read the conclusion, *The Future of the Hawaiian Islands*. Think about how the structure of this article helped you understand the topic.

Writing a Cause and Effect Article
- Choose an event with clear causes and effects.
- Write an introduction that gives general details about the event.
- Write "cause" paragraphs that tell why the event happened.
- Then write "effect" paragraphs that tell results of the event.
- Tell about the end of the event in your conclusion.

2. Choose Your Topic

Now choose an event in nature to write about. It should be an event that changed Earth's surface in some way, such as a landslide or an earthquake. You may find some ideas on the Internet or in books. Be sure to choose an event for which there are clear causes and effects.

3. Research Your Topic

Now that you have chosen your topic, you need to find more information about it. Use several different resources to find the information you need. Take notes as you come across important facts. Organize your information according to whether it is a cause or an effect.

Landslide

Cause: heavy rain

Cause: erosion

Effect: buildings destroyed

Effect: people killed

4. Write a Draft

Now it is time to write a draft of your article. First write the introduction. Give general information about the event, such as when and where it happened, how severe it was, and if people were affected. Write a section on the causes of the event and a section on the effects of the event. Finally, write a conclusion that explains how the event ended or describes possible future effects of the event.

5. Revise Your Draft

Read over what you have written. How clearly have you presented the information? Rewrite any unclear parts. Check against your research that all the facts you have included are accurate. Correct any spelling or punctuation errors that you find.

SHARING YOUR WORK

Create a Cause and Effect Chart

Follow the steps below to turn your article into a cause and effect chart. Then you can share your work with your classmates.

How to Make a Chart

1. Think of a heading.
Your heading should tell what the chart is about. Write the heading at the top of a large piece of paper.

2. Write down the causes.
Write the causes of the event in a list on the left-hand side of the piece of paper. You will not have much room for detail, so you will have to write brief notes. Draw a box around the list.

3. Write down the effects.
Write the effects in a list on the right-hand side of the piece of paper. Draw a box around the list.

4. Draw an arrow.
Draw an arrow across the page, linking the "causes" box to the "effects" box.

5. Illustrate your chart.
Add any diagrams or illustrations to make the text easier to understand.

6. Display your charts.
As a class, pin your charts to the classroom wall. Then move around the room, reading each other's charts. Be prepared to answer any questions about your chart.

Glossary

earthquakes – the effect of tectonic plates moving and causing the ground to shake

effects – changes caused by the action of forces

erosion – the moving of worn-down rock and soil to another place

faults – cracks in Earth's surface caused by moving tectonic plates

forces – causes of movement and change

hotspot – an area of extreme volcanic activity under Earth's surface

landforms – natural shapes on Earth's surface

lava – hot melted rock that pours out of a volcano

magma – hot melted rock beneath Earth's surface

seismic waves – shock waves that come from the center of an earthquake

seismologist – a scientist who studies earthquakes

tectonic plates – large moving pieces that make up Earth's surface

vent – an opening in or between tectonic plates

volcanoes – openings in Earth's surface through which red-hot melted rock erupts

volcanologists – scientists who study volcanoes

weathering – the wearing away of rock over time

Index

erosion 7

eruption 12–13, 16

fault 9, 15

force 4, 7–10, 14

hotspot 10

landforms 5, 7, 12

landslide 9, 12

lava 10, 12–13, 16

magma 10, 13

seismologist 14

surface 4–13

tectonic plates 8–10

vent 10, 13

volcanologist 16

weathering 7